Diaries of Broken Moms:

The Secrets She Carries

by
Clarissa Rose

EVOKE180 PUBLISHING | LAUDERHILL, FL

Copyright © 2023 by **Clarissa Rose**

All rights reserved. No part of this publication may be reproduced, distributed or transmitted in any form or by any means, without prior written permission.

Clarissa Rose/Evoke180 Publishing
Lauderhill, FL
www.evoke180.com

All rights reserved. Except as permitted under the U.S. Copyright Act of 1976, no part of this publication may be reproduced, distributed, stored in a retrieval system, or transmitted in any form or by any means- electronic, mechanical, digital, photocopy, recording, or any other except for brief quotations in printed reviews, without the prior written permission of the publisher.

Printed in the United States of America
Translated by Evoke180 LLC

Diaries of Broken Moms/Clarissa Rose.
ISBN 978-1-7377826-7-4

DEDICATION

This book is dedicated to all mothers, especially my mother, Ms. Connie G. Smith.

ACKNOWLEDGMENTS

Writing this book was an interesting journey. One that took a few years to complete. I was consumed with a rollercoaster of emotions and took many breaks along the way. Only the mothers interviewed, my publisher and his team, husband, and very few friends knew of this project. That is a testament to the level of focus and intimacy this book required.

So I'll start there!

I would like to first acknowledge the mothers who allowed me into their space where we were able to share and navigate through our emotions together. I admire each of your strengths and vulnerabilities. Thank you for trusting me to share your stories. As I began this process, I had no idea how deep, raw, and captivating our collective stories would be or how difficult yet therapeutic the unveiling of our traumas would feel. Writing this book required unashamed transparency and revisiting the inner parts of us that WE, for one reason or another, have masked. However, we did it! We shared our emotions unselfishly and created a nonjudgmental space. Thank you for trusting me to be a part of your process, as you have also been a part of mine.

To my dear husband,

Honey, *you* are my greatest supporter, life partner, and best friend. You continuously shower me with patience, love, and encouragement. I honestly feel that this book would have been further prolonged if it weren't for your daily reminders that I owed it to myself and *all* mothers to bring our stories to light.

Because of the nature of this book, there were many days when my heart felt heavy and many nights that I found it difficult to sleep. In those moments you showed up as an anchor of strength. You covered me in prayer, consoled me as I cried, and remained kind to me even in moments when I wasn't the kindest to you. You have seen my best and worst throughout this journey, but your love has never wavered. You continuously motivated me, and I am forever grateful for you! Thank you for being my Rock.

To my publisher, Mr. Berwick Augustin of Evoke 180,

You were truly a class act throughout this entire process. I told you early on that I intended for this project to be written and published a few years prior to meeting you; however, it all made sense as to why it was prolonged. You were indeed the missing piece of the puzzle. You knew this body of work was dear to me, and you handled it (and me) with such esteem and delicacy. In those moments of wanting to throw in the towel on this project (because of the emotional toll and anxiety that came along with it), your constant reminders that these are stories that people *need* to hear was a tremendous push for me to carry on. Thank you from the very depth of my heart!

To my family and friends,

I am blessed to have the village that I do. Thank you for your continued prayers, love, and support. This especially applies to my parents Connie Smith and Ednal Rose. I wouldn't trade either of you for the world! Since I was a child, you have embraced and fostered the gifts that would shape me into the woman I have become. You supported all of my endeavors without being pushy or intrusive. Neither of you have ever forced your ideas on me regarding *who* or *how* I should be. You embraced each chapter of my life with open hearts and loving arms. I was free to '*be*'! What else could I have possibly asked for?

Last but not least, I would like to acknowledge my children.

Zion and Zamar,

Being your mom is my GREATEST joy! I never knew what it meant to be selfless until I had you guys. You keep me energized and motivated. Each day I look forward to us growing, learning, and exploring together. I consider it an honor that God chose me to be your mommy! A role I don't take lightly.

Zion, you were my very first love at first sight! I admire your zest for life, eagerness to learn, creative mind, and empathic heart. Being your mom keeps me busy, yet centered. You motivate me to become a better me! Know that Mommy believes in you, as I want you to always believe in yourself. You are blessed and a blessing.

Zamar, my precious baby boy! Your newborn innocence represents the purity needed in this world (especially during these times when the world is chaotic). Interestingly, you and this book share a special connection. As I was writing, you were growing inside of me. Some of the experiences I felt while pregnant with you and post-pregnancy are documented in this journal. It has been an interesting ride but all worth it. You've brought such joy and color to our family!

I never realized how quickly time goes by until I had you guys. This is why I maximize each day we share, give tight hugs, invest quality time, and say "I love you!" each opportunity I get. I will forever cherish, love, and support you both to the very end!

Love,

Mommy

Words of Encouragement From the Author

I never knew the level of bravery it took to be vulnerable about your pain, mistakes, experiences, and shortcomings. It takes strength to face your trauma and be unapologetic in doing so. However, I believe that on the other side of it there is a great reward-the reward that comes with letting go of the pain that harbors trauma in your heart and limits your fulfillment in life.

So, I encourage you to reflect on the experiences that hold you back and rid yourself of the shame. I know this is easier said than done. I am also aware that healing can hurt, but the important part is to begin the process, and the first step is being honest with yourself.

I LOVE YOU.

I BELIEVE IN YOU.

I PRAY FOR YOUR HEALING.

AND I WANT YOU TO BE ENCOURAGED IN KNOWING THAT YOUR TEST CAN VERY WELL BECOME YOUR TESTIMONY.

SENDING LOVE,

CLARISSA

Contents

Words of Encouragement From the Author 7

DIARIES OF LOSS — 10

I Awaited You 11
Can I Go to the Special Place? 14
doin it, ALONE! 19
Motherless Mom 23
Stillborn 26
Pass Me Not 28

DIARIES OF NEGLECT — 31

Disregarded 32
Hubby a Hustler 35
Postpartum 36
Status Quo 40
Now 45

DIARIES OF GUILT — 48

Teen Abortion 49
No Justifiable Reason 52
Black-and-Blue Love 55
I Didn't Keep My Promise 57
I Sentenced My Child To DEATH 61
Staying For Them 66

DIARIES OF CHILDHOOD TRAUMA — 68

Rain, Rain, Go Away! 69
Searching 72
Her Lovers Loved Me 74

DIARIES OF WORRY — 76

Black Son...78
How Will I?..80
We Need Each Other (Prayer) 82
Shamefully Broken, but … 84

Closing Words From the Author.................................89
About the Author...90

Diaries of Loss

I Awaited You

*(31-Year-Old married woman.
This would have been her first child)*

....

I still rub my stomach and feel connected to you.
I still wish that I was able to have and hold you,
to share life with you,
to watch you grow into your full self, and to be there for you each step of the way.

And out of nowhere, absolutely nowhere!
My stomach began to cramp with unbearable pain.
I fell in the fetal position and guarded my stomach firmly.
My first instinct was to protect you.

Thursday May 13, 2021, remains the worst day of my life!
I keep having those nightmares…
The ones with your hands stretched out calling,
"Mommy! Mommy! Protect me!"

We didn't get to live a life together,
but our love was intertwined.
My womb was your home.

I rejoiced in every twist and turn,
nudge and squirm, wiggle and roll that you made!

I awaited you …
I was anxious to see how God masterfully crafted you

with features of your dad and me
and our moms and dads.

I awaited you ...
My love for you flowed through every inch of my body.
It coursed through my veins,
pumped through the umbilical cord,
and went directly to you.

I awaited you ...

There's nothing that I wanted more than to hold you in my arms at night and rock you back and forth as I sing, "Twinkle, Twinkle, Little Star."
I had already mentally prepared myself for the sleepless nights and long days.
I knew that you would have been worth it.

My baby,
I awaited you!
I don't know how those movements stopped or why my womb was unable to keep you,
but just know
that until your very end,
Mommy's unconditional love flowed
through every inch of my body.
It coursed through my veins,
pumped through the umbilical cord,
and went directly to you!

PS:
Mommy still loves you.
I still rub my stomach and feel connected to you.
I still wish that I was able to have and hold you and share life with you,
but I will NEVER forget the beauty of waiting for you!

What is the one thing that you have "awaited" that didn't come to fruition? What was that feeling like for you?

Can I Go to the Special Place?

(29-Year-Old Woman. Social Worker. 1 Child)

···

It seems that things have a way of falling apart at the most inconvenient times. I'm aware that in life we all experience some degree of misfortune, but in John's case, misfortune became all too regular. From his mother passing while he was still young to having to live household to household, it all set the precedence for how he would feel about himself and others. John didn't trust many people and was hesitant to let anyone in. He had a fear that if he did so, they would either leave or hurt him.

Throughout childhood and young adulthood, John was misunderstood. In grade school he was labeled "different." He had misplaced anger and emotions that he himself often didn't understand.

But, thank God for football! To him, it was more than "just" a sport. It offered him a sense of belonging, love, brotherhood, and the father figures he yearned for.

When he and I met, it was like fire and ice. I was his cool, his calm. On a surface level, I can't fault people for questioning how or why we got together. All I knew was that our connection was divine. John allowed me to love him, and God allowed me to give John a gift that he loved with his everything—our son. When Lil J was born, so was the joy in John's life. He was the best father that any child could ask for! And to think he was actually nervous ...

He parented our son in a way that I've only seen in movies. They adored each other! After Lil J was born, things were on the up and up. John became more even tempered, started a business, and had a promising view on life. After so many losses, it was finally his turn to experience triumph. His friends and family watched as he was on the verge of scoring the long-awaited touchdown of a fulfilling life.

Then, the whistle blew!

Just as he was about to make his touchdown, the timer on the scoreboard struck zero. His death was sudden, and I was left to pick up the pieces- pieces that I'm still trying to gather, and with voids that are still left to be filled.

Some say that time heals all wounds. Well, I've not been one of the fortunate ones to attest to that. As a matter of fact, with time came more complexity and pain. When John passed, our son was only 11 months, so there was very little that I needed to explain to him.

My main focus was trying to keep myself as emotionally aligned as possible and come to grips with the fact that I'd be raising our son without his father. I always wanted our son to feel his dad's presence, so I never disregarded him. There are pictures of him around the house and we take regular visits at his grave site.

I would tell Lil J, "Let's go, baby, we're going to spend time with Daddy today!"

He'd be so happy! We would decorate his plot, and Lil J and I would play right there for hours at a time. It was comforting to me, because, in those moments, I would feel John's presence, a recharge of strength, and, as strange as it may seem, would feel as if our son was having quality time with his dad.

The real tests came as Lil J got older. He watched other kids curiously during school pickups, at the park, on trips to the grocery store, and even times amongst our family and friends. In these moments, he realized that he was missing something-something that many of them had—his father (in the physical form).

Then, one day, came the question that I dreaded, yet desperately tried to prepare for. We were driving home from school, and out of nowhere he asked, "Mommy, where is my daddy?"

This moment was even more intense than I could have prepared for. My heart dropped, and my eyes began to water. My body felt so numb that I couldn't even formulate words.

"Huh, Mom?" He was waiting for an answer.

I pulled the car to the side, looked into his curious eyes, and said, "Daddy is in a special place." He looked out of the window and looked back at me. "But why doesn't he ever pick me up from school or come to our house?"

I said, "Because Daddy has to stay at the special place, but he is always with us in spirit. Even though you can't see him, he's aaaaalways here!"

"Okay," he said blandly.

My heart ached badly. I saw that it was confusing for him, but his four-year-old mind was still trying to process and understand.

When we got home, I figured having a little movie night would take his mind off of it a bit, and it seemed to be working.

Once the movie had finished, Lil J laid tucked in his bed. With his arms folded across his chest, he looked up at the ceiling and asked, "Mommy, can I go to the special place to see daddy?"

RIP Johnathan Aiken November 28, 1991–June 22, 2018

What would your response be to Lil J asking, "Mommy, can I go to the special place to see daddy?"

What words of encouragement do you have for this mom?

doin it, ALONE!

(28-Years-Old Trying her best but still hurt)

It really hit me today…
Father's Day…
My son gave ME a shout-out.

I never really talk about this cause I don't wanna fall under the stereotype of the "bitter baby mama" or "poor me."
When it's all said and done, I made my bed so I have to lie in it…
And that's exactly what I'm doing.
So this ain't for sympathy or clout, I'm just tryna let my feelings out!

See, I was raised on survival, not love.
My mama wasn't much help because she needed some mending and raising her own damn self!
I ain't had nobody to look up to! NOBODY!
Everyone was just doing the same ole thing, getting the same results, and passing on the same messed up BS to dey kids.

But me? I just wanted something different.
I would always tell my homegirls,
"Look this ain't it! It can't be! When I have my kids dey ain't gonna go through this shit!"

When I was about 17, almost 18, I started dating Reggie.
He wasn't perfect, but he never hit or cursed at me.

Where I'm from, a dude who didn't do those things was like Prince Charming, and that's exactly what he was to me.

We was inseparable!
When you saw him, you saw me.
I was on cloud nine. Shoot, Cloud 100! (*chuckling*)
Finally, I wasn't living by survival but experiencing true love.
Reggie was my EVERYTHING... No family, no friends, no anything! Just US.

With him, I had all I needed!
Until I got KNOCKED UP, that is.

Reggie wasn't ready for kids, and, if I'm honest, me either.
We were young and didn't have a pot to piss in.
But what was I supposed to do?
I ain't gonna pretend that I didn't think about having an abortion, but I just couldn't go through with it.
I was determined to give my baby all the love that my mama couldn't give me.
I was gonna do it with or without Reggie, and that's exactly what I did.

It wasn't my baby's fault that I wanted to be grown and didn't have my stuff together.

But I'll tell you one thing, my son ain't being raised on survival.
I'm there EVERY step of the way!
Every disappointment!
Every game!
Every practice!
Every rise!
Every fall!

I'M THERE! PRESENT! Front and center! With LOVE!

Hell yeah, even after all this time it still hurts losing the guy that I loved and that my son doesn't have a father in his life, but he's gonna be just fine.

People always say a woman can't raise a man,
but when a woman has no choice, you'd be surprised what she can do!
I'm doin it ALONE and I'm doin it well.

Do you feel that people who are raised on love grow up differently than those raised on survival? If so, how?

Motherless Mom

(35-Years-Old/Married/Two children/Middle class/Nurse)

•••

I take lots of pictures with my children so that if I pass while they are still at a tender age, they will have enough memories and photos of us to last a lifetime.

When my mom passed, I was only four-Years-Old. My dad raised my older brothers and I. He was the best! My dad spoke of my mom often. This really helped, being that I had little memories of her. I was told that she was the most loving mom there was. Dad always said that she made it clear to everyone (including him) that her children came FIRST!

I was told that even at age four, I would wake up constantly throughout the night. Despite long days at work, evenings filled with festivities with us, preparing dinner, and making sure we were settled in for bed, my mom would comfort me each time with no complaints. As she hummed sweet lullabies, I would lay my head on her lap and fall asleep.

Everyone describes her as a 'fun' mom. She loved taking us outdoors to play. She would kick the soccer ball with my brothers as I would play around in the grass.

My oldest brother, Joshua, was seven when Mom passed. He tells us of so many great memories. One of my favorites that he shared was when our dad arrived in the driveway, mom would take all three of us to a hiding place, and Daddy would walk throughout the house looking for us. When we heard his footsteps coming close, we would dash out in front of him shouting, "Boo!" It would scare him each time, my brother says. Or perhaps he was great at pretending.

When I look at family photos and see my mom, I can imagine what her voice must have sounded like, her fragrance must have smelt like, and see the pure love that she had for us in her eyes.

Now that I have children of my own, oftentimes I'm saddened by the fact that my mom is not here to teach me how to be a mother, the kind of mom that she was to us.

I strive to embody each memory that I've gathered about her and incorporate her style of mothering towards my children.

When they were babies and woke up throughout the night, I lovingly sang them sweet lullabies. I take them outside to play and have picnics on the grass. When my husband arrives home, we hide while he tries to find us as we anticipate the moment to playfully frighten him.

As I write, I'm realizing that though my mother is not physically here, she is guiding me in spirit. She didn't give up on me. She simply left way too early.

Being that this mom does not have her mom to share the motherhood journey with, what advice would you give to her about motherhood?

Stillborn

(25 years old/Christian/Married)

I grew up with the ideology that God makes no mistakes and not to question Him.

Well, I now question if there is even a God. I'm not proud of that, but I just don't understand how a God who is supposed to be so merciful would allow me—not a perfect person, but a strong believer—to conceive and carry a precious seed for nine months in vain!

It was love at first sight and a final farewell all at once.

Today would have been my baby's birthday. As the day goes by, I try to make it a celebratory occasion, but my heart still aches. This kind of pain is beyond emotional. I can physically feel my heart shattering into pieces. I haven't been the same since January 13, 2017. How? Better yet, why?

I can't erase the labor pains that I felt, the push, and holding my lifeless baby girl in my arms. My heart is shattered. But, for what it's worth, I will continue to celebrate her birthday every year. I just wish that this pain would go away.

Do you believe in the idea of *not* questioning God as to why things happen? Why or why not?

Pass Me Not

(59-Year-Old mom/Devoted Christian/He is her only son)

• •

Setting: At Church before prayer meeting
Singing: "Pass Me Not, Oh Gentle Savior"

"Pass me not, O gentle Savior
Hear my humble cry;
While on others Thou art calling,
Do not pass me by.
Savior, Savior
Hear my humble cry;
While on others Thou art calling,
Do not pass me by."

Note: Mother was overcome with tears, worship, and prayer. I got permission to journal during the process.

My God! Yahwehhhhh! Oh God!
My heart aches, dear God
Oh God, my heart aches!
God, I have faith in you like Ruth, Heavenly Father, and the patience of Job.
But my heart is heavy, dear God!
I've tried everything that I can and everything that I know, but I see no changes.
God, I have raised the son you have blessed me with like Hannah raised Samuel, dear God.
He was raised in your temple and in your Word.

You said in Proverbs 22:6: "Train up a child in the way he should go: and when he is old he will not depart from it." Well, God, I've trained, I've prayed, and I've fasted.
Yet the enemy has found a way to seep into his spirit, causing him to live a life that is not pleasing in your sight!
Oh God!!!! Why God?
I am your faithful servant! I am demanding the spirits that are not of you to be casted away, RIGHT NOW, in the Name of Jesus!
Satan shall NOT have my son! The plans of the enemy shall NOT prevail!
Dear God!

[She falls on her knees before the altar, looks upward, and tries to control her breathing.]

She begins to sing again:
"Pass me not, O gentle Savior,
Hear my humble cry;
While on others Thou art calling,
Do not pass me by.
Savior, Savior
Hear my humble cry;
While on others Thou art calling,
Do not pass me by."

Father, my son has strayed , but just as the Prodigal Son, I pray that he returns home new! Washed clean. White as snow…

At this point, I discontinued writing to console her

If you were able to have a conversation with this mother what would you say?

Have you ever been deeply disappointed because your child was living a way that you disapproved of? How did you cope with it?

Diaries of Neglect

Disregarded

(66-Year-Old Retired Southern Mom)

I love my son dearly.

I worked hard, I mean HARD, to give him the best I could and put him through school.

But we don't talk anymore.

A phone call from him is rare since he got married, had kids, and started his career.

I don't want any of his money or take up too much of his time,

but it would be nice to see pictures of my grandkids, even if he doesn't bring them by.

I'd love to make him a home-cooked meal on holidays just like old times.

Well, minus the "meat," because, last I heard, he's vegan now.

Today is his birthday. Yep! Boy, how time flies.

I called to wish him a happy birthday. He didn't answer.

I tried calling his wife's phone, but neither did she.

On my son's phone, I left a voice message,

"It's mama calling again. I hope everything's fine.

I can't believe you're thirty four-Years-Old now! My, how time flies!

I know it was many years ago, but I was thinking 'bout your tenth birthday.

Remember? It was the first time you had a birthday party.

Everybody was there! Even your fifth grade teacher, Ms. Sinclair.

We sang happy birthday to you.

When you cut your Ninja Turtle cake,
You gave me the first piece.

That cake was so sweet! Good lawd, it tasted like diabetes!

You hugged me tight and said, 'You're the best mom!'

Well,

I just…

I just want your hug again, son.

I just want to see the love in your eyes again.

I just want…

Okay. Bye-bye now.

Mama loves you.

I'll try calling again…

tomorrow."

As a mother, have you ever felt neglected by your child(ren)? If so, in which way?

How are you coping with that feeling?

Hubby a Hustler

(34-Year-Old former 'City Girl')

....

Today was a LONG-ass day! *Rolls Eyes*

Laying here missin' bae.

People refer to us as "Relationship Goals" all the time, because they see the crib, cars, jewelry, and the clothes.

But Lord knows it ain't easy, and everything comes with a price tag.

Our price is hubby always being gone.

Jr. is getting older…

Baby girl be wanting her dad to hold her,

but I can't even trip, 'cause he out there chasing dat cake,

making sure me and the kids straight!

When I was growing up, I went through the same thing with my pops… He stayed hustling.

I don't want our kids going through the same shit.

So, I told hubby, with this money we have to start flippin' it…

Just so he could free up his time a bit…

As for me, I try my best to not complain,

but it would be nice to have a little bit more time with my man! *Flips Hair*

Anyways…It is what it is!

Postpartum
(23-Year-Old-first time mom)

While pregnant, I was the happiest woman ever! I would even receive compliments from strangers telling me how much of a "glow" I had.

I read numerous books on motherhood and attended Mommy and Me classes (even though my baby wasn't born yet).

I bought her the cutest little clothes and all of the toys and books that promoted early development.

Despite my cravings for pineapple Fanta soda and slices of green apples dipped in hot sauce *chuckling* I curved them all! I was determined to be as healthy as possible so that, while breastfeeding, my baby would get the "top-grade" milk.

I WAS PREPARED!....

Then, the moment I had been waiting for came.

The doctor handed her to me... I looked at her in my arms, and I FROZE!

I felt numb...

So many thoughts ran through my mind.

I didn't know what to do.

All of the preparation from those books, videos, and classes went out of the window!

I didn't have that "happy" feeling that I anticipated.

Then it was time to breastfeed, and she didn't latch.

Well, honeyyyyyyyyyy!!!

That was the beginning of a volcano of emotions that erupted!

I cried uncontrollably. Despite the nurses' reassurance that many babies had a difficult time latching, I took it as a PERSONAL failure, along with everything else that was to come.

As the days went on, my sadness increased.

In short,

I felt that I had given my child life, but I was losing mine.

The center of attention was on the baby; meanwhile, I was silently screaming for help, wondering how it was possible for everyone to not see that I was drowning…

I felt neglected.

Sounds selfish of me, doesn't it?

I know!

That's why I typically don't share my feelings with anyone.

Anyone except my baby… I'm sure that she felt it.

As I breastfed her, I cried.

As I changed her diapers, I cried.

As we started our day, up until I put her to sleep, I cried.

When I looked in the mirror, my reflection disgusted me. It was as if I became unrecognizable to myself.

I was always irritable and sad.

I couldn't sleep.

I barely ate.

It was difficult for anyone to support me, because my roller coaster of emotions made it impossible to articulate my needs.

I didn't know what I needed.

I didn't want it to seem as if I didn't love my child…Because I did, yet sometimes it felt like I didn't.

Confusing, right?

I know!

My daughter was, and still is, the best thing that ever happened to me, but I wasn't able to fully wrap my mind around the mixture of emotions that I was feeling.

Over time, I became even more critical of everything that I did as a mom.

I had moments of wanting to run away, but, in the same breath, couldn't be without my baby.

I even thought about dropping my baby off to some kind of foster home where they could match her with someone who could be better for her than me…

Selfish, right?

I know!

But I also knew that she didn't deserve a mom who was straight-up depressed!

I loved my baby intensely, but often thought of how much happier I was before giving birth to her.

Wait…

That reallyyyyyy sounds selfish, right?

I know!

The battle with my thoughts became so overwhelming that I asked my sister to keep her until I cleared my mind a bit.

It's been three days now, and a part of me feels good to be away, but the other side of me is filled with the guilt of neglecting my baby…

After having your child, did you experience postpartum depression or didn't feel like "yourself?" What was that process like for you?

....
....
....
....
....
....
....
....
....
....
....
....
....
....
....
....
....
....
....
....

Please speak with your doctor or expert if you are experiencing signs of Postpartum Depression

Status Quo
(Retiring Highly Influential Medical Doctor)

••

I spoke to a group of aspiring doctors at the University of Miami today. It was informative, yet brief, due to my busy schedule. After speaking on the importance of vaccination, I opened the floor for a few questions. All but one was related to the topic at hand. However, that particular question is what led me to this point.

The student asked, "Dr. Thomas, I want to start off by saying that you were my inspiration to become a doctor. I have read all of your books, watched many of your interviews, and attended seven of your seminars. My question is, knowing all of your professional accomplishments, would you be willing to tell us more about yourself, personally? About your upbringing, children, and hobbies?" She then went on to say, "I hope that I'm not being too intrusive."

I paused.

This question was a bit off-putting, seeing that I speak very little of my personal life.

Oddly, today I felt open to sharing.

My response:

"As you are aware, I have been in the medical field for the past twenty-three years. However, I came from very humble beginnings, which I won't elaborate on, for the sake of time. I have been married for twenty-nine years. My husband is an attorney and legal advisor to a mayor in one of the cities in South Florida. As far as my hobbies are concerned, I enjoy traveling, so much so that we have several vacation homes in various parts of the world. I also enjoy reading and wine tasting. Then of course there is the humanitarian aspect of providing scholarships and mentorship to aspiring medical students who perhaps came from a similar background as me."

She then asked, "What about your children? They must be proud to have a mother as successful and impactful as you!"

I apprehensively paused.

"That'll be it for today. All the best to you all." I then exited the auditorium.

As I drove to my next engagement, I thought about her question the entire time.

Are my children proud of me?

I never quite thought of that.

Well, I provided them with a wonderful life!

They never lacked attention. We've always had a full-time nanny and housekeeper who would play with them, prepare their favorite meals, assist with homework assignments, and chaperone them on outings with friends.

My husband's schedule was just as demanding as mine. Hence, our help would often attend PTA meetings and extra-curricular activities on our behalf.

Both my son's and daughter's first vehicles were Mercedes Benzes.

They were able to access my credit cards by the age of ten.

Sure, my career was and remains demanding, but I made certain that their needs and wants were met and that someone was always there for them.

Once I got home that evening, the question of whether my children are proud of me continued to linger.

I called my son (who is a university student).

Me: Derrick, How are you? I need your complete honesty. Are you proud of me?

Judging by his pause I could tell that he was caught off guard

Derrick: What do you mean by that?

Me: I mean exactly that. Are you proud of me?

Derrick: Yes, how could I not be? Look at all of your accolades. You're one of the top doctors in the country, you have traveled the world, and have friends of influence. You are an inspiration to many!

Me: Yes, but are you proud of me as your *mom*?

He paused. I could tell that he went into deep thought.

I remained silent as I anticipated his response.

Derrick: Well, I don't know. (*Pause*) You aren't the typical mom. Growing up you weren't really there. If I'm honest, not much has changed.

(When he said this my heart dropped, and for the first time in my adult life, I felt as though I was a failure.)

Derrick: But you and Dad made sure we had a good life. We were privileged. We had a lot of "stuff," and I'm grateful for that. It's now that you asked that question I'm able to say that though all of those things were amazing, we needed YOU! We wanted our mother more than we wanted things. We wanted you to be involved, to cheer for us in the stands at our games. We wanted you to play and laugh. Like *truly* laugh. Do you know that I don't know the sound of your genuine laughter? Oh, and dinnertime! It would have been nice for us to sit at the dinner table and tell you all about our day, about our friends, and how we felt. Ashley and I knew that your job was very important, but I guess we just wished that *we* were *most* important, that time with us was a priority.

Me: Honey, I'm sorry. Perhaps it's too late to make up for lost times?

Derrick: Perhaps, Mom. Perhaps

As you reflect on your own life, do you feel that you have ever prioritized other things (career, relationships. etc.) above your children that may have left them feeling neglected?

....
....
....
....
....
....
....
....

Do you agree or disagree with Derrick's perspective that it is too late for them to "make up" for time lost?

....
....
....
....
....
....
....
....

Now

*(31-Years-Old mom.
Dealt with many hardships throughout her life)*

••

I've been tired for a while now. My smiles are becoming more and more difficult to fake. Dark thoughts are chasing me, and I'm in desperate need of an escape.
My chest is heavy and my lungs are full. It feels like I'm gasping for air. Constantly tussling between spiritual and emotional warfare.

I've been self-medicating and meditating, but neither of them left me with any resolve.
I've prayed for a breakthrough, comfort, and calm, but those prayers have gone unanswered.
I even spoke to a therapist. She said that we'd first have to get to the root of it. But when we began peeling back the layers, the pain just got greater. Like damn! I didn't realize how much there was to this.

Today, it's a lot heavier than usual. I'm at my breaking point NOW. I've reached out to everyone, hoping that someone would have the right thing to say, but nobody answered my call. No one!
I feel so alone and disconnected…
The only thing that keeps me fighting is my kids, but as of recently, they aren't even enough.
My kids are gonna be hurt. I know they will!

They'll probably hate me for life for what I'm about to do, and I wouldn't blame them.
Maybe one day, as they get older, they'll understand.
Never mind, I take that back.
I never want them to understand. I never want them to be so unsettled with living that they could see how someone would not want to be here anymore.
What I do hope is that they know that my choice is not their fault and that they were the only people in this world that I ever truly loved.

When I drop them at Mom's house this evening, I'll hug them extra tight and a little longer because it'll be the last hug we'll have left to share…

If you were the person that this mom was calling for a listening ear, what would you have said?

Diaries of Guilt

Teen Abortion

(She is reflecting on her 15-Year-Old self.)

....

I often wonder if God forgave me.

I try to convince myself of the reasons that He may have, like:

"God is a merciful God…"

"I was young…"

"I was a good girl who just made a mistake…"

"If God can forgive murderers, surely He can forgive me…"

But then it hit me, "Am I not a murderer?"

How does He forgive that? I can't even forgive myself.

I honestly didn't want to do it, but I had my entire life ahead of me.

It was the summer before tenth grade, and all the other girls were talking about how good sex felt. I was the only odd ball who couldn't relate.

So I tried it. I did it with my friend's older brother.

It wasn't pleasurable at first, but I tried it again… and again.

They were right! It was good!

Almost addictively good, if I'm honest.

As I got more and more comfortable with him, we started having unprotected sex.

Did I know better? Of course I did!

My mom was a cool kinda mom. She would always talk to me about sex and stressed the importance of using a condom. Her favorite line was, "I can't tell you not to have sex, but if/when you do, pleeeeease protect yourself."

She even went as far as purchasing a "just in case" stash of condoms that she put in my dresser.

But I got caught up and went against my better judgment.

Just like that, I got "caught."

Once I missed my period, my older cousin took me for a pregnancy test.

There I was, young and afraid, sitting on the bathroom floor sobbing.

I sat there for at least an hour trying to process it all.

My initial thought wasn't to get rid of it. It was more so *how* will I be able to take care of it?

For five days I sat with these thoughts. I didn't tell my mom, my cousin, the guy… I didn't tell a soul.

On day six, my mind was made up.

I had to get rid of it! The details of how I went about it are too gruesome and shameful to revisit, and maybe that's a part of why it still haunts me to this day.

Now that I'm older, I often think about how things would have been if I kept the baby. Maybe it wouldn't have been as bad as I thought it would have, or, perhaps, it would have been.

Either way, I still haven't forgiven myself. I just hope that God forgave me.

Now that you are an adult, what would you say to your younger self about the mistakes you've made?

No Justifiable Reason
("Happily" Married Housewife)

I made a mistake a few years ago.
An enormous one!
Not even sure why I did it.
I've tried everything not to think about it,
but it stalks me like a nightmare, even when I'm awake.
It hovers over my conscience like a dark cloud.
It follows me like a shadow.
Ever heard the song "Little White Lies" by Tanya Stephens?
It goes,
"I see your daddy in everything you do
And if you could talk, I'll bet you'll talk like him too."

She then goes,
"But he can't be your daddy, I hope you understand
The man who thinks he's your father
Is a much better man."
Deep breath

That's the part that gets me!
Those lyrics stab at my soul each time.

I can't forgive myself…
I feel so grimy…disgusting…nasty…
Mainly because I had no justifiable reason.
He's a great husband!
A provider, protector, and confidant.

At no fault of his, I made the ultimate betrayal as his lady.
Not a day goes by that I don't contemplate uncovering the truth.
But, how could I?
He loves our baby.

Bedtime stories and diaper duties are all his.
At doctor visits, he asks more questions than me!
He provides her with presents and his presence.
He prays over her and speaks positive affirmations into her life daily.
They even have little tea parties.
It's the cutest thing you'd ever see!
He loves our baby…
I want to uncover the truth,
But, how could I?
What hurts me even more than hurting him is the fact that my daughter is growing up with a false identity.
Her features are becoming more defined.
She's not looking like him and only has the slightest resemblance of me.
But how can I tell him the truth?
He loves her dearly.

If *you* were her, how would you confess? Or would you not?

Black-and-Blue Love

(Mid- Fifties. In a 30 year relationship with her children's father)

As a mother, I never want to see any of my children hurt. Even though they're all grown, I still worry about them. When they hurt, so do I. But this had to be the most painful experience yet.

I always knew that my youngest, Krystal, and her boyfriend didn't have the most healthy relationship, but I didn't know just how toxic it was.

Last night she called me crying and asked to stay at my place for the night.

When she got here, I couldn't believe how badly she was beaten. She didn't even have to tell me who did it. I knew it was him.

I told her that she had to leave him!

She looked me in my eyes, wiped her tears, and said,

"But you didn't leave Daddy… Remember the times he kicked and dragged you all over the house floor, giving you black eyes, a broken nose, and bruises all over your body? But you STILL STAYED! Yes, Drew gets jealous and loses his temper, but he's not nearly as bad as Dad was. So don't judge me when you let Daddy do even worse to you!!!!!"

So essentially, it was me that taught my daughter how to "love" even when it's black and blue…

Thoughts…

I Didn't Keep My Promise

(Single hard working mom. Mid-thirties)

Growing up, my family structure wasn't much different from anyone else who was around me. My mother worked hard to keep food on the table, so, understandably, she often seemed tired, stressed, and worried.

Sometimes the lights would go out, and we'd run low on groceries, but Mom tried her best, for a woman who was underpaid, undervalued, uneducated, and unmarried.

Dad stopped by from time to time, but as the years went by, memories of him became more and more vague.

Well, except for those trips to Mickey D's!

I remember those moments vividly.

It would be him, Jermaine, Vonte, Toya, and me.

Each time was like déjà vu.

As he bit into his Quarter Pounder with Cheese, simultaneously he'd say,

"Jermaine, I heard you dropped twenty nine last game! Yo mama said you scored the highest on the team! Das whatsup, man!"

Jermaine, who wasn't much of a talker, would typically give a head nod, but his eyes spoke loudly.

They said, "I wish you were there."

When Dad would drop us home, he always left the car engine running.

"All right, y'all be good. See y'all soon," he'd say.

My brothers and sister would reply, "See ya, Dad!"

Me, on the other hand,

I wasn't so swift to bid him good-bye. It just wasn't that easy for me.

I would unzip my denim backpack and hand him a stack of letters that I wrote.

Each one represented each day that I didn't see him.

We hugged.

He left.

Those moments were always bittersweet.

Sweet, because I always looked forward to seeing him.

Bitter, because I never knew when we would see him again. If he couldn't be with us every day,

I would have gladly taken every weekend…

If he couldn't be with us every weekend,

I would have been okay with it once a month…

I didn't mind having pieces of him, so long as I had *him*.

As I got older, I made a promise to myself that my kids' childhood would never be like mine.

That I would never be so overworked that I couldn't help with homework or do school drop-offs or pickups.

I promised that their dad and I would show up to everything and anything that they are a part of.

That we would sit at the dinner table and converse about each other's day.

That we would have family game nights and BBQs.

I made a promise that inconsistency, as it relates to their parents, would be nonexistent.

That we would rewrite the generational DNA of a broken family being the norm.

I made a promise!

Fast-forward…

Today, as I sped from my second job to my son's basketball game,

I left the engine running.

I tried to catch the last second of the last quarter.

I missed it…

I missed his shot…

I missed his game…

On the car ride home, he asked to stop at Mickey D's.

As he ate his Quarter Pounder with Cheese,

I said, "I'm proud of you, Son! You scored the highest on the team!"

He didn't say much, but his eyes spoke loudly.

They said, "I wish you were there!"

I didn't keep my promise!

Explain the most difficult promise that you've broken as a parent.

Have you forgiven yourself? If so, how? If not, how are you coping with the guilt?

I Sentenced My Child To DEATH

(58-Year-Old mom.
Opening up after seven years since losing her son.)

⋯⋯⋯⋯⋯⋯⋯⋯⋯⋯⋯⋯⋯⋯⋯⋯⋯⋯⋯⋯⋯⋯

When I would watch the news, there would always be a report about someone who was involved in a robbery or homicide as a result of gang violence or some other criminal activity.

Oftentimes, it would be followed by a mother crying her heart out and talking about how much of a good person her child is/was. And just like most people, I would give those moms the side-eye. Talking to them through the TV screen, I'd say, "So that guy who just killed an innocent child in a drive-by is a 'good guy?' That person who just broke into someone's home and stole everything they worked hard for is your 'innocent son?'"

That was my reaction every single time!

Until I became "that" mom...

Once my son became a man he was no stranger to the law.

He created a name for himself that traveled through the entire city.

But I was MAMA.

So each time he got into trouble, I was there.

And with each bailout, he would promise me that this time would be the last time.

So, with the most recent court case, I made up my mind that I would not come to his rescue.

I showed up to court for support but was prepared for whatever his judgment would be.

When he was found guilty, I literally felt as if I was on the verge of having a heart attack.

He looked back at me, and when I looked in his eyes, I didn't see what everyone else saw…

I didn't see a "monster." I saw my son and MY SON needed his MOM.

So I pleaded with the judge to allow me to sign his bail.

She rubbed her forehead, removed her glasses, and looked down for a brief moment as she sighed.

When she looked up, she looked deeply into my eyes as if she was searching for my soul.

She said: "I am not talking to you as a judge. I am speaking as a mother. I see your pain, and I empathize with all that you have endured having a son in and out of the system. While Darius is eligible for bail, I would advise you to put deeper consideration before making your final decision."

Once she was done speaking, I looked at my son one more time and responded, "Thank you, Your Honor, but this time will be the last time."

She silently stared at me, put her glasses back on, and took another deep breath.

We proceeded with the bail process.

Four-hour break before I could continue to write.

So, three days later, before he left home, I said, "D, please don't get into any trouble. My heart is weak now. Mommy can't take it anymore."

He kissed my forehead and said, "Mommy, stop worrying! I told you that was the last time… Love you."

Well, he told me the truth. It was the last time, because that evening my baby was killed.

He wasn't doing anything to provoke it. Just the wrong place at the wrong time.

Sometimes, even when you've changed, your past still finds you.

Two days later before I could continue to write. This is so hard to do.

When I got the news, the first person who came to mind was the judge, who looked me in my eyes as if she were trying to get to my soul and advised me to reconsider.

If only I had listened, my son would have been alive today. He was only going to be sentenced to two years in prison. But, because of me, he was sentenced to death.

One week later before I could continue writing.

So, because of who my son was, all of the local news reporters came to interview me.

How did I start the interview?

"My son was a good guy. He was just misunderstood."

And I could say that because, to *me*, he was.

My son never disrespected me.

Never raised his voice. Never talked back.

Never left the house without kissing me on my forehead. Never brought any drama to my house.

Not even a fly could come near me in his presence.

He reminded me of how beautiful I was. We would dance our little two-step on the living room floor. And as he spun me around, I couldn't help but smile.

Until I tried to lean back in his arms! He would say, "Hold on nah, Ma! You a whooollle lotta woman! You have to warn me before you do that!"

We would both laugh until our eyes teared. *Smiling*

So, to *me*, he was a good guy… He was my loving son and my heart!

Nothing is the same without him.

I feel like I'm living, but dead inside.

And before I closed his casket at his funeral, I said, "Mommy is sorry that I couldn't save you, but I love you even in death."

How do you empathize with this mom?

Explain the most difficult regret you've had to live with as a parent?

Have you been able to forgive yourself for that decision that has haunted you? If so, how? If not, how are you coping with it?

Staying For Them

(Mother of two. Married for 8 years)

At this point my marriage is a pretense. Each day I put on a facade of happiness, though I'm actually feeling an emptiness that aches. Our marriage has run its course, and at this point, it feels like we're roommates. I've tried everything to rekindle what we once had, but there seems to be no mending in sight.

When we speak there is hardly anything to talk about other than the kids. The common interests that we once shared have shifted, we sleep in separate bedrooms, and even our steamy love making has become just occasional "sex"—and, on my end, more of an obligation rather than a desire.

Recently, I've been thinking about divorce. The thought alone gives me a sense of guilt because it's something that I vowed to never do. It's just that, in my heart, I know that this season is over. My husband hasn't admitted that his feelings are the same, but, based on his actions, I know that they are.

We are both unhappy.

Even though I have accepted the reality that our marriage, in its *authentic* form, is done, the only thing that's keeping me in it is our kids. All they know is us being together, and I've heard far too many stories of how divorce can cause negative effects on children.I wouldn't want my selfish decision to cause them emotional instability. We have a pretty solid system going as it pertains to them, and I don't want to mess that up.

So I guess I'll just stay for their sake.

Do you believe in "Staying for the sake of the children" or would you divorce? Elaborate on your response.

Diaries of Childhood Trauma

Rain, Rain, Go Away!

Each time it rains, my three-year-old daughter innocently sings, "Rain, Rain, Go Away!" To her it's simply a song, but to me it brings flashbacks and memories of *that* night.

Rain, rain, go away!

I was about seven or eight at the time. While sleeping, I felt the sheets being slowly pulled down from my body. When I looked up, it was my mom's boyfriend, Don. I froze! It happened quickly, yet slowly all at the same time.

He kissed my neck while rubbing my barely developed breasts. Then he pulled my Barbie underwear aside and penetrated me with his finger while making moaning sounds.

Rain, rain, go away!

I was numb!

I couldn't scream…

I couldn't move…

Even my tears were at a pause.

What was happening!? Perhaps my mind was too busy trying to conceptualize "WHY!?"

Rain, rain, go away!

He never made eye contact with me. As a matter of fact, he kept his eyes closed the entire time. When he was done, he covered me with the sheet and left the room. I focused my eyes on the hallway light that was shining in through the door crack. As soon as the numbness broke, I packed a bag of clothes and ran outside, only to be met by the RAIN!

Rain, rain, go away!

I was mortified! I didn't know where to go or what to do. So, I sat underneath the mango tree in front of the yard, fretfully waiting for my mom to come home. She worked overnight. By the time she arrived, the rain had stopped. She met me sitting underneath the tree. I was drenched in both water and tears. I tearfully told her what happened. She immediately asked, "But... Did he put his penis inside of you?" I said, "No, Mommy." She took me inside and told me to take a shower and get a few hours rest before school. We never spoke of it again. Ever.

Rain, rain, go away!

I'm now thirty seven-Years-Old, and when it rains, *that* night still haunts me as if it were yesterday.

What is a more effective way this mom could have handled this unfortunate situation?

Are there any unresolved traumas that you still carry with you? If so, how are you coping with it?

Searching

(Mother of two. Exploring how her childhood led her on an unhealthy pursuit of love)

....

No mother's affection
No father's protection.

No reassurance of my intelligence and beauty
No quality time spent
No one really knew **me**.

No example of how I should be treated
No one to talk to when needed.

No feeling of belonging.
Truthfully, that's all that I've been longing.

So here I am,
through all of life's stages
searching…
for love
in all the wrong places.

Take a moment to reflect on your childhood. How has it influenced (positively or negatively) the path that you have taken as an adult?

Her Lovers Loved Me

Explicit language
(Raw and furious as she revisits this experience)

•••

To this day, I hate my so-called mother for not giving a shit 'bout who she brought 'round me!

Every Tom, Dick, and Harry she was messing 'round with either did or tried to mess around with me!

I don't understand how she let dem motherfuckers violate me like that!

And now she wanna give me these too late- fake ass apologies. Talking 'bout she was young and on drugs and shit.

I ain't tryna hear dat shit!

But she damn right though! SHE is sorry! A sorry ass excuse of a mother.

She FUCKED my life up!

Got me scared to bring any motherfucker 'round my daughter because of what she let dem fuck ass niggas do to me!

But see, the difference between me and her, is I would do time 'bout mine.

I HATE that bitch!

How do you feel about this mom's stance as it relates to her unwillingness to forgive and hatred towards her mom? Can you relate?

Diaries of Worry

What is the greatest worry that you have as a parent?

Black Son

There was an overwhelming level of anxiety the moment I found out that we were having a boy...

I think the common desire for most parents is for our children to be safe, treated fairly, and have a decent shot at life. However, as parents of black children, especially of black sons, we are constantly reminded of the devastating reality of what being a black male in America comes with. History has and continues to show that they are not "safe" or treated fairly. In fact, it is the complete opposite. As I raise my young black sons, I am by no means oblivious to the cruel world that they face. I yearn desperately for a change, but based on the constant murders of unarmed black men, a flawed criminal justice system, and systemic racism embedded in this country, it doesn't look very promising.

What's most disheartening is having to have "the conversations" to prepare them as best as I can for this cruel and unfair world.

My black son...

Be cautious not to be at the wrong place at the wrong time, because if something goes wrong, more than likely the blame will be placed on you. When you dress, please stay away from wearing hoodies, because this can appear "threatening." Yes, my black son! I know it is just a hoodie, but hoodie+black+male=murderer, thief, and criminal.

My black son!

Before you enter the car, be sure to have your driver's license with you, check your head and tail lights, make sure that all of your car signals are working, and your tints are not too dark. As a matter of fact, don't put any tints on your car windows!

Do all you can to minimize your chances of being pulled over by the cops, because a routine stop can result in you losing your life.

Oh, my black son!

I know that this may sound ridiculous, but Mommy is just trying to protect you! I know that it shouldn't be this complicated, but it is!

My black son!

I'm sorry that your skin has to be ten times as tough and you have to move twenty times more cautiously…

I'm sorry that you are not truly "free"…

My black son,

I would be lying if I said that I don't worry about you.

I pray for you more than I pray for myself.

I know it's a bit overbearing when I'm constantly calling to see if you've made it to your destination,

but I just want to know that you are safe…

My heart worries for you… My black son!

And so long as your skin is black and their hearts are cruel, I will always be on guard when it comes to you.

How Will I?

(34-Year-Old single mom with two low income jobs)

••

Times are hard, and I've got three mouths to feed. It was tough before Covid, but it's even harder now. The cost of living is going up, but the pay is not.
As the kids get older, the more they wanna do things.
And so do I!
So, it hurts each time I leave them deprived...
Deprived of a summer trip or even an outing to an arcade or movie...
Deprived of a toy they've been wanting or even a little birthday party...
Because, quite frankly, anything other than an ABSOLUTE NECESSITY is considered LUXURY...
Because I gotta make a choice between *do we have fun* or *do we eat*... and that's just our reality...

I'm penny-pinching and getting a little assistance, but the bills are plenty...
And now there's inflation and talks of a recession...
I'm trying not to worry, but it's getting really depressing...

How?
I ask myself this question day and night.
How will I provide?

This is what worries me.

What has been the greatest hardship that you have faced as a parent? How did overcome it or what would it take for you to overcome it?

We Need Each Other (Prayer)

Dear God,

There's so much going on in the world.
Each day, it seems that more and more people are dying and leaving their children behind and that worries me.
So, God, my biggest, sincere, and most-humble prayer is that you KEEP ME.
Keep me for my children, because we need each other.
I don't want to leave them in this world without a mother's love.
I don't want them having to figure things out all by themselves.

God, keep me!
Keep me because no one will love them the way that I do.
No one else will stick by their side through the triumphs and the trenches like I will!

God, keep me!
Keep me because the world is so cold, and they need the warmth of their mother's arms.
The plans of the enemy are so strong that they need someone who would go to war for them both physically and spiritually, and that person is ME!

God, keep me!
Until they are equipped to carry on this journey of life without me.

Amen

Write a prayer dedicated to your child(ren).

Shamefully Broken, but ...

(The Author's Story)

"What have I gotten myself into?"
"The doctors warned me. How could I have been so careless?"
"This guy seems nice now, but we've only been together for a short time.
What if he switches up on me?"
"I haven't healed completely from my past relationship. Did I move on too soon?"
"My life isn't where I want it to be. I'm a college drop out with no career and no money".
 And... And... And...

I remember it like it was yesterday.

"Congratulations! Guess who's having a baby!?" exclaimed the excited nurse

I looked at her with eyes filled with disbelief, mouth speechless, and body numb. Her cheerfulness turned into a state of confusion. "I'll give you some time alone," she said as she left the room.

I've been here before.
And with both pregnancies ending in miscarriages, I know that I wasn't mentally, physically, nor emotionally prepared to experience that again...

Each time left me feeling...
inadequate and weak
incapable of being a "woman."

After leaving the clinic, I was a nervous wreck! I pondered for hours before telling my boyfriend that we were expecting. He and I spent about two weeks thoroughly weighing out the pros and cons. Our final decision was to have an abortion. This decision was heart-wrenching for both of us.

Leading up to the appointment, I cried each day. I barely ate or slept. Having an abortion was against our belief, but we felt that we *had* to do it. Especially considering the fact that the cause of my previous miscarriages was never rectified. The guilt of knowing that this could have been avoided is what hurt me the most.

On December 3, 2016, Dro and I drove to our appointment. The drive was dark and heavy. Each traffic light we approached was red. I wondered if those were signs that we should *stop*. At each light, we looked at each other with worrisome eyes. My stomach felt as if it was tied in a knot. My head was throbbing intensely. The air felt thick and suffocating. My heart felt as if it was beating too fast for my body. This was by far the most daunting feeling that I've ever experienced.

When we arrived at the parking lot of the abortion clinic we just stared at each other, but exchanged no words. I took a deep breath and quickly opened the door. Oddly, there was a beautiful duck near the door entrance. SHE WAS STILL, YET VERY AWARE.

I then walked into the clinic and was greeted with, "Hello! Welcome!" I was caught off guard by the irony of someone being so lively at a place where many pregnancies were terminated. I was given a form to fill out, but I could barely make out what it said. My sight was blurry from the river of tears flowing out of my eyes.

I made it as far as writing my name before I began sobbing. There it was: **Clarissa Rose**. I wrapped my arms around myself, trying to soothe my nerves, but it didn't work. I couldn't believe I was actually doing this.

I looked out through the blinds wondering why my boyfriend hadn't come inside yet. He stood there staring at the duck. I closed the blinds and continued filling out the form.

Just as I was about to complete it, he walked in and said, "Come on, let's go."

I looked at him confused.

"Come, let's go!" he repeated impatiently.

I was absolutely puzzled, but I got up and left.

Once we got outside, Dro drew my attention to the duck and how she sat there protecting her eggs. He looked back at me and uttered, "Nah! We can't get rid of it! I know what the doctors said about you not being able to carry a baby and I know we don't have all our sh*t together yet, but we'll figure it out."

I, in tears, nodded in agreement and we left.

Now the journey officially began and what a journey it was!

Once we found an OB-GYN who specialized in high-risk pregnancies, he automatically placed me on bedrest and weekly doctor visits. Throughout the pregnancy the cervix pain and spinal discomfort felt unbearable. Because my cervix was so fragile, there wasn't much certainty that I would be able to carry the baby past six months. For this reason, we didn't share that I was pregnant with friends and family until we were in "the clear."

With the physical pain along with not having my village to support me emotionally, there was a feeling of brokenness and darkness that was difficult to shake. I was completely miserable and oftentimes second guessed if we made the right choice.

Just as I was at my breaking point, there was a supernatural shift that took place! Within the remaining months of the pregnancy, I was able to re-enroll in graduate college, my boyfriend's career advanced which helped us become more financially stable, and each week the baby progressed well. After nine months, we gave birth to a healthy baby boy! Zion was my very first love at first sight and the 'son-shine' that cleared the dark clouds away. He was worth it all!

Fastforward, I began a career in Education that I was passionate about, my then boyfriend is now my husband, and we now have another precious son, Zamar.

We couldn't have asked for a better outcome.

YET!

There was an immense guilt that still lingered, which actually led to the start of *this* book. The fact that we were going to abort Zion haunted me like a nightmare for years. I've prayed continuously, asking God to rid me of that feeling, but it persisted! Then, one day, out of desperation to release all of the emotions built up inside me, I decided to do what I've always found most comforting. Write! I sat in my room and wrote for hours. I wrote in detail about all of my pain, trauma, and guilt. I allowed myself to be completely vulnerable. And guess what? It was such a liberating feeling!

This is the first time that anyone other than my husband and I knows of that experience. Perhaps that's one of the reasons why this journey has felt so lonely. I've never shared it until now.

To me, my journal symbolizes a safe space, a space that doesn't judge or correct. So I thought to myself, *I can't be the only mother that yearns to release her pain, trauma, and secrets.* This encouraged me to introduce the idea to mothers in my circle, social groups, parenting groups, and to absolute strangers to allow me to share their 'journal.'

Together, we hope it becomes a tool that more women will use to help find solace, peace, and healing.

After reading the book, how are you feeling?

Which journal entry resonates with you the most? How so?

Closing Words From the Author

Dear Moms and Readers,

I assembled these journal entries for YOU…for US! As I began this process (over four years ago), I had no idea how deep, raw, and captivating our stories would be and how difficult yet therapeutic the unveiling of our secret traumas would feel. Writing this book required unashamed transparency and revisiting the inner parts of us that we (for one reason or another) have masked. However, we did it! We shared our emotions unselfishly and created a nonjudgmental space. Perhaps, because of this, those who will read our stories will learn from our experiences, become more hopeful in the midst of their own traumas as they move toward healing, and/or empathize with the painful experiences that many mothers carry.

Thank you for not only reading but also taking the time to write and reflect. Most of you probably experienced an array of emotions. However, I hope that your main takeaway is that you are not alone, that there are so many individuals who carry hurt inside, and it is okay to release it. I intended for this book to be a safe space for all of us.

Thank you for your support and love.

I am grateful to have you be a part of my tribe.

Should you ever need assistance in connecting with a tribe that is willing to support you, please connect with me so that we can seek the best resources for you.

Sending Love,

Clarissa

About the Author

Clarissa Rose is an English Language Arts educator, poet, and writer. She studied at the historical Florida Memorial University where she co-founded the renowned "Chapter 3 Poetry Troupe." Clarissa has conducted numerous poetry and writing workshops throughout South Florida over the last several years.

Ms. Rose credits her dedicated mother for her profound appreciation for women. After becoming a mother in 2017, Clarissa developed an even greater level of respect for the strength of moms. This admiration motivated her to collaborate with organizations that provide support, mentorship, and resources to mothers, especially moms with low socioeconomic status and who were victims of domestic violence.

Clarissa was born in Miami, Florida, but raised on the beautiful Island of Nassau, Bahamas. She considers her faith and family to be most important to her. She enjoys spending time with her husband, Sandro, and sons Zion and Zamar. *Diaries of Broken Moms: The Secrets She Carries* is Clarissa's first published book.

Contact

✉ clarissarosespeaks@gmail.com

Ⓕ Facebook: Clarissa Rose

⊡ Instagram: clarissarose_speaks

www.ingramcontent.com/pod-product-compliance
Lightning Source LLC
Chambersburg PA
CBHW042129100526
44587CB00026B/4231